T0198945

WHEN
GOD
SAYS
NO

CHUCK MCLAMORE

authorHOUSE®

AuthorHouse™
1663 Liberty Drive
Bloomington, IN 47403
www.authorhouse.com
Phone: 1 (800) 839-8640

Published by AuthorHouse 11/09/2018

ISBN: 978-1-5462-6557-1 (sc)
ISBN: 978-1-5462-6556-4 (e)

Library of Congress Control Number: 2018912013

Print information available on the last page.

CONTENTS

FOREWORD

"I know you're able and I know you can
Save through the fire with your mighty hand
But even if you don't
My hope is you alone
I know the sorrow, and I know the hurt
Would all go away if you'd just say the word
But even if you don't
My hope is you alone"

Those lyrics are to the chorus from a song called "Even If" by Mercy Me. Those lyrics are a marvelous summary of how we should feel about God. Many of us believe that God is all knowing and all powerful. We trust this because His Holy Word tells us that. So when bad things happen to us in life, we often blame God. We attribute control of everything to Him so He either caused something to happen or allowed it. We struggle with understanding why He lets things happen to us that seem unfavorable. Often times we think we're supposed to learn something from the situation but we struggle to figure out what that lesson is. But right in the middle of going through whatever challenging thing it is, we have to keep the right perspective. We have to constantly remind ourselves that even if God doesn't take the pain away, He is still God. Even if He doesn't help us the way we want or expect that'll make us feel better, He is still God. He still loves us and knows what's best. We have to force ourselves to trust and believe in Him, when it's hardest to do so. This book is my attempt to aide your understanding of how to do that. But before I try to help you, I feel it's necessary for me to inform you of the reason why I wrote this book. The first chapter is my personal story of the situation that made me truly analyze how we as people can prepare for, endure through, and respond to God answering no to our prayers.

ONE

OUR STORY

When my wife was pregnant for the first time we prayed for the well being of her and the baby. We had faith that God was going to take care of us and we never thought something bad would happen. We prayed multiple times a day every day. Among other things, we constantly prayed for the health, strength, nourishment and growth of both my wife and the baby. We did this even while my wife was having constant nausea and vomiting from week 6 on throughout week 20 of the pregnancy. I was optimistic that her health would improve as time went on because we heard from various sources that's what happens. But it never got better. We did plenty of research and heard many things. Turns out that every pregnancy is different and some are just tough to deal with throughout the whole time. This seemed to be one of those just tough to deal with pregnancies. In our 20th week of pregnancy on a Thursday we went to the anatomy ultrasound appointment and found out the sex of the baby. It was a girl and we named her Madison. That Saturday morning my wife started bleeding and we went to the hospital. We found out that she had a weak cervix and that the baby was going to be born. But since it was just 20 weeks, they would not try to save the baby because it was too soon. Madison's lungs weren't developed enough yet to breathe well and her eyes were still fused shut. Those were the things we remembered but there were more reasons as well. At that hospital a baby has to be at least 22 weeks for them to attempt to keep it alive. We were devastated! I literally couldn't believe that our baby was only TWO WEEKS away from them trying to save her. Instead we were faced with the reality of our first child being born and dying the same day. The staff at the hospital told us that when a woman has a weak cervix the miscarriage usually occurs between 16-20 weeks of the pregnancy because that's typically when the weight of the sac becomes too heavy. There is no way to know whether a woman has a weak cervix until the miscarriage happens. It's not necessarily hereditary, but it can happen in successive generations. Among the other myriad of feelings I had, one of the main ones was confusion. I was so confused at why God allowed this to happen to us.

As I mentioned earlier we prayed and had faith about the well being of our baby. It never occurred to us that something like this could happen. We were mainly concerned about the health of my wife and Madison because of the excessive vomiting my wife was doing. The only thing we were concerned about was if Madison was getting enough nourishment and our doctor assured us she was. While we were in the hospital the staff allowed us to keep Madison's body for the night. They wanted to monitor my wife's progress and they planned on discharging us Sunday afternoon. It was at this point in the hospital where I had to ask myself how I'd respond to this. It just didn't make any sense to me why God allowed that to happen to us. I felt like we were being punished for something. Up to this point I thought that as long as my wife and I were trying to live right things would go well. (By living right I mean trying to obey God's word.) Of course we weren't and still aren't perfect but I thought we were doing well enough to avoid a tragedy like this. So many thoughts ran through my head while in the hospital. I wondered if God allowed this to happen as punishment for my fornication that I was guilty of committing in my past. I thought He was taking this pregnancy away from us because we weren't as grateful as we should've been because of my wife's health challenges. I questioned how genuine our prayers were. I questioned our faith. I questioned our lifestyles. Those were just some of the thoughts that I had that were torturing me throughout our time in the hospital. I looked at several choices that were before me.

1) I could lash out at God because of my anger.
2) I could continue to feel helpless and depressed.
3) I could try to find reasoning behind it.
4) I could try to fake being content until it worked.
5) I could just trust God that He knows best.

What I ended up doing was continually going back and forth between all of these options as well as others. It was an emotional roller coaster like I'd never experienced before. Not only was I dealing with my emotions, but also my wife's and mother's emotions as well. I had to try my best to be there for them as well. But I didn't want to. I wanted to just think about me. In the situation I didn't see it as me being selfish. I saw it as just doing what I needed to do because I was in the midst of grieving. But as a man I know that women are more emotional than men normally are so after about an hour I tried to focus my attention on my wife and mother. It's extremely difficult to compartmentalize like that when you really don't want to. But that was a time where I had to do what was best for others instead of myself.

I just couldn't help but be confused as to why God allowed this to happen. Now I know that God is not the author of confusion, but of peace (1st Corinthians 14:33), so I tried to wrap my mind around why this happened and how I should feel. Along with that knowledge, I also know that we don't always find out why God did or didn't do something. We as people are so far beneath Him and we can't understand everything about Him and His will. He only lets us know certain things (Deuteronomy 29:29 & Isaiah 55:8-9). So sometimes in life the answer to a question is "you don't need to know that". At this time I needed clarity and I only knew one place to get it, God's word. Leaning and depending on God is most critical when we're weakest. When we're at our weak points and we realize we can't control everything, we're forced to look at the one who can. As much as I was hurting at the time I remembered the phrase that Job uttered thousands of years ago when he lost so much at one time. Job 1:21 "And he said: "Naked I came from my mother's womb, And naked shall I return there. The LORD gave, and the LORD has taken away; Blessed be the name of the LORD." I repeated that phrase over and over again. Then I remembered Matt Redman made a song out of those lyrics called "Blessed Be Your Name" that I had heard on the radio often. So I started singing that song also which was verbatim quoting the same verse. To this day I am convinced that those words helped me keep my sanity. In 50 hours from Thursday afternoon to Saturday afternoon my wife and I went from the joy of learning the sex of our baby, to learning that Madison wouldn't live. Obviously we aren't the first couple to have to deal with losing a child and there are plenty of other couples that have lost children in worse ways. However, none of that knowledge actually helped provide comfort in that time. The only thing that brought me a tiny bit of solace was remembering that a part of God's ability as Creator is that He gives and He takes away and that's just a part of who He is. I had no other choice but to accept that and move on. If I had allowed myself to continue to dwell on my feelings, they would have overwhelmed me and there's no telling what would've happened. I had to let my mind be focused on how and why my faith has grown so much over the years. I studied and taught God's word for many hours over the previous seven years and I couldn't throw away all that scriptural knowledge and those many faith building experiences just because I was emotionally broken.

I didn't put this story in here to try and say that I handled that situation perfectly because I know I didn't. My reason for including that story is to be transparent. Usually when I preach a sermon I like to let the congregation know the inspiration of the lesson, where it came from and why I felt it could help someone. I feel that when people know the details of what they're being taught it will have a lasting affect on them. Also in a group of people no matter the size, there is almost always someone there that can personally relate to the subject matter. It can help them gain a different perspective of something they went through in the past, something they're currently going through, or something they'll face in the future. I firmly believe that after choosing to still trust and depend on God, one of the healthiest things my wife and I did in the days after this was being transparent with each other. We talked about every thought and feeling we had that we might have been okay with not sharing with each other. There were some things shared that could have potentially fractured our relationship with each other and or our relationship with God. But transparency produces a level of vulnerability that we as people usually aren't comfortable with. What usually makes people comfortable is showing the best version of themselves to other people. Being uncomfortable is good because it leads to growth. Being transparent is like getting a load off of you. By not carrying it, you feel lighter. That old saying "no pain, no gain" has so much truth to it. It can be applicable in any situation in life. Often times it's used in a physical or working out environment. After lifting weights and exerting physical energy the muscles are sore because they're growing. That's a great parallel lesson to the spiritual working out we do as well. We're told bodily exercise profits a little, but godliness is profitable for all things" in 1ˢᵗ Timothy 4:8. Physical exercise is good for our physical bodies but no matter how much exercise one does, their body is still going to deteriorate. Spiritual exercise for our spiritual body will never deteriorate. Spiritual growth is life's most important aspect because it's the only part that will last forever. We can grow spiritually by positive situations like studying God's word and trying to live by it daily. Or we can grow spiritually by negative situations by being caused pain when we don't avoid or overcome sin. Growth doesn't exclusively happen because of pain, but oftentimes pain causes the most affective growth. When growth comes from pain we must embrace it and not hide from it or fight it. When we embrace the pain we can learn from it effectively. We don't go through the pain just for no reason, we must learn from the pain. No good parent disciplines their child just for the fun of it. They do it with the intent that the child learns a lesson from it. As parents people raise their children with the intent of that child becoming a good adult. Typically no one sets out to raise the next Hitler. One of the goals is for your children to not have to depend on you when they're adults. Because there's going to come a time when you're not around and you want your kids to make good decisions based off what you taught them.

As a parent God treats us the same way. And even though God never leaves us, we frequently leave Him. But with God raising each of us there's no becoming

18 and leaving home. There's no going off to college or moving out and getting a job. We're always going to be His children and He's always teaching us. For some reason we as people learn well through pain. It'd be great if we learned the best by hearing and following directions. If we learned by the examples of others whether good or bad, that'd be great as well. We could learn what to do or what not to do by looking at the examples in other people's lives. Learning those lessons could be especially helpful when the specific subject is something that commonly happens to people. We could save ourselves much pain, but we often don't. Learning from the examples of others is one of the main lessons to understand from studying the Bible. God gave us the Bible with the specific purpose and intent of us actually using it. The information it contains is for us to learn how much God loves us. Apart of God's love toward us is helping us know how to live life how He wants us to so we can be pleasing to Him in this life and the next.

TWO

EXPECTATIONS

In the world today there is one prevalent form of teaching that is seriously shortsighted. Far too many people have been taught that when things are tough all they need to do is pray and have faith. It doesn't matter what type of church or religious organization you're a part of, many people have heard that from various people, via several media outlets. Whether it's word of mouth, T.V., radio, books, magazines, the internet, or by some other means. This teaching is widely taught and accepted. However it's limited in the sense that it gives people an incomplete understanding of how to deal with situations in life. You may be saying to yourself, "if the teaching is so wrong, why is it so popular?" That's a fair point, to which I'd respond that the teaching isn't really wrong as in incorrect, it's just incomplete. And when a process of steps is given incompletely, the outcome will not reach it's full potential. It's like only giving someone half of a recipe to bake a cake. The cake isn't going to taste right because it didn't have all of the necessary ingredients. Telling people that praying and having faith is all they need to do to get through situations is setting them up for disappointments. If you start with the wrong expectations for how something is going to unfold, you'll be less acceptant of the actual outcome.

Most people have the understanding that praying is talking to God and that having faith is to trust and believe in God. James 1:6 talks about asking God for something in faith, without doubting. So if you have a situation that you want resolved you may think that if you talk to God about it and really believe He will resolve it, then it will be done. Well, not always. We as people have a handicap called selfishness. It shows up at times in our lives and we don't even recognize it. We tend to think that the world revolves around us. So when we are in a situation, we're usually only seeing it from our perspective. Even when we attempt to see things from someone else's perspective, we usually just see it as our perspective if we were in their situation. That's completely different than if we know someone well enough to know their tendencies and characteristics that would help us to accurately reflect on how they think and respond. God is able to see things from unlimited perspectives. Let's say you have applied for a job and you're praying that God lets you get hired. From your own perspective you see the benefits of that job and how it can help you. However, God knows if there is someone else that needs that job more than you. Also, there may be some negative effects of having that job that you are oblivious to. So if you don't get the job how would you respond to that? Would you be able to accept that maybe God has something else for you? How long would you hold on to the disappointment of getting passed over? Would you be able to be happy that you didn't get the job because you trust God knows best? Would you dislike the person who got the job? One of the ways our thinking gets defeated is by not allowing ourselves to ask those tough questions. If we don't ask ourselves those tough questions we aren't forcing or challenging ourselves to grow. But even if we do ask ourselves those tough questions we have to do it with the proper motives. The basis of our motives must be for understanding and grow. The basis shouldn't just be to vent and get out frustration. That can be a part of the reason because venting can be emotionally healthy when done correctly. The only way we can vent correctly is by exercising self control. Self control is one of the most important aspects to human life. It is applicable to every situation in our lives. By being aware of our ability to control our thoughts, words, and emotions, we can unlock previously neglected areas of our faith that are desperate to get out. Let's look at this some more.

Often times when something happens that we perceive as undesirable to us, we get mad at God because we attribute control of situations to Him. Being mad at God looks different depending on who the individual is, their experiences and understanding. By being mad at Him, you submit to Him having power and control over situations that you aren't capable of controlling. So the very act of being mad at Him, acknowledges His greatness. We must use our self control to increase our level of reverence for God. Reverence is having respect and fear for God. The level of reverence someone has for God will greatly influence how people react to what they perceive as God saying no to their prayers, or just when the outcome of a situation is different than what we thought would be best for us. Someone with a lower level of reverence for God will tend to blame Him for things that happen. While focusing on ourselves, we don't have the mental capabilities to see things the right way all the time. In that instance we're handicapped by selfishness affecting our viewpoint whether we recognize it or not. We struggle with being humble enough to know we don't always have the best ideas and thoughts for our lives. The main reason is because we fail to accurately equate how our life relates to the lives of so many others. Far too often, when we focus on ourselves we ignore so much else. We tend to give less effort in paying attention to how situations affect others. While having a high level of reverence can help us to accept that He knows best and we shouldn't worry about what could've been.

Being mad at God is different from being mad at a person for several reasons. First, He's smarter and more powerful than any person can ever be. Also, since we can't see God physically it's more difficult to direct our anger. When we're mad at a person we can direct our anger easily. We can yell at them, hit them or do something else that can affect one or more of their senses. I'm not saying those are good ways to handle it, just that those are options people can choose from when they feel the need to "get back at someone". The fact that we can know and see the results of affecting them can provide temporary petty/immature satisfaction to us. It's okay to have anger as long as we handle it correctly. We can handle it in emotionally healthy ways by expressing it. That's what we're doing when we vent to someone about something. But venting is not the only way of getting out or expressing our anger. Some people do unhealthy things to express anger such as smoking or drinking. Others try working out, hitting a pillow, singing songs, reading or writing something, etc. There's a plethora of good, clean, emotionally and physically healthy ways of getting out anger when needed. Being mature enough to not feel like we want to "get back at someone" is key though. When we're at the point where we don't feel like that with people, we'll be better equipped to feel that way about God also. Constantly forcing yourself to remember who He is and what He's capable of is important. In the "microwave society" that we live in nowadays we want instant results. So it's hard enough to control our emotions waiting on an answer from God for something we're praying about. The difficulty of the task is raised when the answer we get is no. Wanting to show our frustration is the main thing that gets us into trouble. We have to get to the point where we realize that being mad at God is not an option. There isn't a legitimate reason to think or feel that getting mad at God actually helps anything. The fact that we would even allow ourselves to direct our anger towards Him is an obvious manifestation of our feeble, limited minds.

Let's look at the example of Naaman from 2nd Kings 5:1-14. Naaman had leprosy and heard about Elisha the prophet that could heal him. So he went to Elisha expecting a certain outcome. Not only did he expect to get healed but he thought about the exact way it would get done. Not only did Elisha not heal him the way he thought, Elisha didn't even speak to him directly but rather sent his servant. Then to add insult to injury, he was told to wash in the river Jordan seven times. Naaman objects upon the basis of knowing "better" rivers that he could wash in to be clean. Verses 11-12 show that these series of events infuriated Naaman so he left. His expectations not being met almost lead to him missing out on his healing. He had to be convinced by one of his servants to obey Elisha's advice of how to get cleaned. He made Naaman think that if he was prepared to do something great to be healed, then why not do something simple to be healed. The statement his servant makes is a microcosm of what gets us off track often times in our relationship with God. We make the simple things difficult and the difficult things simple. Life can be as simple as just obeying what God says in His word. There was nothing particularly special about the Jordan river. What was special was that God commanded that specific river. Naaman was thinking about the physical cleanliness of the river as opposed to just obeying God's word through the prophet Elisha. Since he didn't see anything special about the river he struggled to accept the command because of his limited selfish perspective. Further more he didn't know that the Jordan river was special to God. Years later that's the river that John the Baptist baptized people in, including Jesus Christ. It's amazing how God uses people, things and events to do His will. It's almost as if God is playing a massively elaborate game of connect the dots.

How often do we do exactly what Naaman did? We as people tend to let ourselves determine how a situation is supposed to play out. Then when it doesn't go as anticipated we respond negatively. We have to accept that we don't always know the best way for things to happen. Our mentalities are so limited but we tend to overstate their abilities. We think we're so smart, but we're really not. We need to force ourselves to be humble enough to be content with the fact that we don't know everything. Even when dealing with our own lives, we don't know what's best for ourselves all the time. God created us and put us in this three or four dimensional realm. Without getting too much into science and math just know that there's not really a consensus on if it's 3 or 4. There's a debate on whether or not time should be considered the fourth dimension. So with us being three or four dimensional creatures we are incapable of being aware of any higher number of dimensions. How many dimensions are there, 5, 10, 50, 100? Only God knows the answer to that because He is not bound by the restrictions and limitations that we are. So because of that reality we have to accept that He knows best. He knows how our situations will affect others.

There's an interesting scene in the movie 'Bruce Almighty' when Jim Carrey's character gets God's powers. People's prayer requests started coming to him and he started hearing voices. He tried to give attention to each and answered some of them but they just kept coming in. Frustrated with the realization of how time consuming answering prayers was going to be he just answered yes to all. That made things so much worse. The city was chaotic and several absurd occurrences happened. One of the events was that 1,100 people from the same area won the lottery. (Bruce only heard prayers from a small area of Buffalo, New York.) Even though that's just a movie I really feel like it's an accurate description of what would happen if God always said yes to our prayers. Millions of people pray for all sorts of things for various reasons, many of them being selfish. Although our selfishness isn't always of malice intent, it's rooted in the fact that we mostly think of ourselves. Controlling our expectations for how a situation will play out is an extension of controlling our thoughts. We need to be more conscious of how we can control our thoughts. The concept of controlling our thoughts is simple, but the application and execution of it is difficult. For example, we all have things "pop" into our mind randomly whether it's song lyrics, movie quotes, past events, etc. But obviously there are certain times where if a thought pops into our mind we have to make sure it doesn't marinate because it's not suitable for the situation. It's not always a vulgar or mean spirited thought, just not fitting for the specific situation. So if you're having a conversation with your supervisor at work, that's probably not the best time to be thinking about a Michael Jackson song. The truth is we can control our thoughts as much as we want to. But we have to have the proper desires and motivation that will influence us to want to do what's right. So if we're capable of controlling our thoughts while talking to our supervisor, we can control our thoughts when thinking about God. That may seem like a big jump to make, but it's true. It's not about being affected by the situation, it's about letting our character dictate how we will handle situations. Whether we accept it or not, we pick and choose how much effort we give to controlling our thoughts. We just have to do a better job of being more aware. Our expectation for how God is going to work in our lives begins with what we allow ourselves to think. When we pray for something we should definitely believe and have faith that the prayer will be answered. But who, what, where, when, why, and how of that answer is up to God. We're just supposed to trust that He knows best with all of those aspects of answering the prayer. When we make up our hearts and minds to do that, then we set ourselves up for handling different situations better. However the situation unfolds won't have such control over us if we first have control over our expectations. We'll be equipped enough spiritually, mentally and emotionally so that we handle the situations how God wants us to.

THREE

SITUATIONS

Accepting responsibility for our actions is something we as a human race have had trouble with since the beginning of time. In Genesis 3 when God confronted Adam with eating the fruit, Adam didn't say "yes God I ate and I was wrong." His response to God about eating the fruit was "the WOMAN whom YOU GAVE to be with me, SHE gave me of the tree and I ate" (Genesis 3:12). At the time Adam only knew God, Eve and himself. I find it fascinating that he deflected responsibility and shifted blame to literally everyone else he knew at the time. Instead of admitting his wrong he focused on the wrong of others. The problem with us deflecting blame from ourselves to someone else is that we negate our own growth as a person every time we do it. One of the most healthy and profitable ways to grow as a person is to learn from our own mistakes. We have to perform a self assessment and realize what we did wrong so that we can try not to keep making the same mistakes over and over again. We need to be our own toughest and most honest critic. That's the point Jesus was making in Matthew 7:3-5. Focus on yourself not others because that's what you can control. It can be difficult to recognize the difference between God putting you through a situation and you going through something that you put yourself in. The only possible way to know the difference between the two situations is to stay in tune with God's will. The more we understand His will, the better we'll be at using our spiritual discernment to see the difference. Things can be very clear because our humility won't allow us to neglect the responsibility we need to take for our actions. Scripture contains several examples of both types of these events. By learning and understanding the similarities and differences between these occurrences then we can compare those to times in our lives. When we compare our lives to the examples we see in scripture it will aide us in knowing whether the situation we're going through is something God is specifically putting us through, or if we're just in it because of our decisions.

Sometimes we go through things that God specifically puts us through in order for us to grow in certain ways. In Genesis 21 when God told Abraham to kill his son Isaac, God was testing his faithfulness and obedience. God promised Isaac to Abraham and Sarah 25 years before he was born. They desperately wanted a son to be the heir. Then after waiting all that time, having the son and raising him for years, God says to sacrifice him. Imagine the emotional stress Abraham was going through while still obeying God. I'm sure he was confused but he still trusted that God knew best. Hebrews 11:19 shows what Abraham's thought process was and gives us a glimpse at his willingness to sacrifice Isaac despite all the potential reasons not to. Turns out God didn't really want him to kill Isaac but Abraham only knew that because he was obedient to God and was about to do what God told him. Abraham probably wouldn't have learned the lesson had he immediately denied God's request or begged God for him to sacrifice something else. He had to go through the physical act of displaying his trust in God by obeying the command. Then God provided another sacrifice after Abraham proved his obedience. This situation is an exceptional example of how God provides for us if we let him. When we make up our hearts and minds to just trust and obey Him and not worry about the consequences we glorify Him. Not only do we glorify Him but we also live more freely and less stressful. Our thought process should be "I'm going to do what God says and everything will work out how He wants them to because He knows best". If we're adamant enough to think like that then our actions and lifestyles will display that as well. While that was a good example of trusting and obeying God, here's a bad one.

Sometimes we go through things that are our own fault and we're just dealing with the consequences of our decision making. Jonah the prophet is mostly well known because he was swallowed by a huge fish for three days. But the lesser known part of the narrative is a prime example of what can happen when we do what we want to do and don't trust and obey God. In Jonah 1:2 God told Jonah to go to the city Nineveh and tell them about their wickedness. Jonah was of the Israel/Hebrew nation and Nineveh was one of their enemies so he chose not to go. Verse 3 says he tried to flee from the presence of God. He knew he was being disobedient so he wanted to get away from God. He paid to get on a ship with some mariners and as they were traveling a terrible storm came on the water. The mariners tossed things overboard to lighten the load and they each started calling on their different gods for help. They found out that Jonah was the cause of all the trouble so they asked him who he was. In verse nine Jonah's answer to them is "I am a Hebrew; and I fear the LORD, the God of heaven, who made the sea and the dry land." That's an astonishing answer considering it came from someone who was only there because of his disobedience to the one he said he feared. Jonah suggests that they throw him off the boat and the storm will calm but at first the mariners don't do it. But then in verse 14 these mariners who previously had their own gods that they followed, cried out and prayed to the one true God. He was thrown overboard and the storm calmed. Many people think that getting swallowed by the fish was his punishment, but it was actually his salvation. In Chapter 2 verses 3-5 Jonah describes himself being surrounded by water. If the fish didn't swallow him, he would've drowned. The fish saved him from drowning to death. After it spit him up he finally went to Nineveh like he should've in the first place. After hearing Jonah warn them the people actually repented. Jonah was actually unhappy with their repentance because of their past sin. Jonah was actually one of if not the most successful prophet in the Bible in terms of the people responding to his message. The mariners who he sailed with recognized the one true God. And the entire city of Nineveh repented from their wickedness. He was unable to see the people of the city through God's eyes that they should have forgiveness. God wants sinners to turn from their sin and He wants the people who have already committed to Him to help with that endeavor.

There's going to be times in life where we just won't know why God allowed something to happen. We have to discipline ourselves to accept those times for what they are. It takes a great deal of humility to do that but we should embrace that because humility helps us get closer to God. There's an exchange between God and Abram (Abraham) in Genesis 15:8-18 that is very complex. What God tells Abram to do doesn't seem to make any sense whatsoever. Throughout Genesis Abraham shows a history of being obedient to God and just doing what He says. This particular passage supports that observation. There is a lot of information present that we can speculate what it means but the text does not give us an explanation. This is just one of many examples all throughout scripture that shows us we don't need to know everything with God. In Genesis 12:1-3 God tells Abram to leave the land he and his family lived in to go to a place that He would show him. God didn't even tell him where to go but Abram still went. There is no hesitation or questioning on Abram's part at all. God doesn't have to explain to us His reasons for us going through things or Him wanting us to obey Him. Sometimes while going through tough situations we try to think about things to help us get through them. We like to tell ourselves that if something we don't understand is happening then God is going to use it for our growth. While it's good to think like that we have to understand that growth comes in various ways. Often times we go through things that are our fault and the tough situation we're enduring is a direct result of our poor decision making. We have to be humble enough to admit when we're wrong and that we're suffering for it. The truth isn't always nice and pretty so we do ourselves well to appreciate the times when we're being punished. Tough times force us to grow because we tend to be vulnerable when we're weak. We also tend to be more willing to ask for and or accept help from others when we're weak. Depending on God when we're weak is easy but the hard part is continuing to depend on Him during the times we're not weak.

FOUR

DISCERNMENT

Whenever there's a problem present in life there are surface issues and root issues. The surface issue is a smaller issue that is easily seen and understood. The root issue is often unnoticed but is more detrimental because it's a problem with the foundation. A surface issue is someone who's living paycheck to paycheck. The root issue is they lack self control to budget their money in a disciplined manner. A surface issue is a child that misbehaves at school. The root issue is a lack of respect for authority which starts in the home. A surface issue is health problems caused by smoking cigarettes. The root issue is a lack of seeing value in life to live healthier. Knowing the difference between surface and root issues is vital to every aspect of life. There are some things that if we commit ourselves to getting better at doing, they'll help us in multiple areas of our lives. There's the foundation, and then things are built upon the foundation. If the foundation is weak and unstable, whatever is built upon it will also be weak and unstable. Jesus mentions this at the end of the Sermon on the Mount in Matthew 7:24-29. Understanding where issues come from is the first thing that we need to recognize. But after recognizing the situation we have the responsibility to use the knowledge correctly. It's easy to say that we need to recognize what situations in our life mean but it's hard to do. There is no cookie cutter approach to having discernment in our lives. It can look different to different people and in the various situations that arise. But there is one question that if we honestly ask in any situation will lead us in the right direction. Does this please God? No matter what the situation is, if we're faced with a decision we can ask ourselves that question and get closer to using our discernment correctly.

Having discernment can look different in different situations but there is one commonality that's always present. Looking at situations the way Jesus did. Jesus always looked at situations from a heavenly perspective. He was always concerned with what pleased God. When He was faced with a decision towards another person He always looked at it with eyes towards heaven. In other words, how can I help this person get to heaven? In every decision we make in our own lives and especially when in junction with someone else that's the question we need to ask ourselves. It's a wide ranging question that will literally help every situation be better. Every decision we make in this life gets us either closer to or farther away from heaven. We can't let other people influence us to the negative so badly that we affect our relationship with God because of them. Likewise, we can't be the negative influence on other people and affect their relationship with God. By asking ourselves how we can help people get to heaven, we force ourselves to think of the long term impact on everything. Not only does it force us to think of our own well being, but about the well being of others as well. We should think of long term impacts because everything has one. There are long term impacts to our lives as well as others. We're largely people of habit so most, if not all actions we take are either continuing an existing habit or forming a new one. So in order to improve our discernment during situations, we need to build the habit of thinking about long term impacts of ourselves and others.

Many people think about what's best for them before they think about what's best for someone else. Even when thinking about what's best for someone else, we can look at the situation from the wrong perspective and get the wrong conclusion. For example let's examine a fairly popular situation like a friend or family member that has a job but asks you for money consistently. Let's say they ask you for money to pay their light bill. Your initial thought is probably, that them having lights is important so that's a legitimate request. You might have a follow up question and inquire why they need the money from you. Let's say their response is they ran short on funds or something of that nature. But then you find out they are being careless with their money and not budgeting wisely. So while deciding on whether you should give them the money you think to yourself that

God says "it's better to give than to receive" (Acts 20:35). Often times it's good to stop right there and not over think the situation. However it's important to consider the broader spectrum of the situation. What are the long term impacts of you helping them in this capacity? We need to make sure that we're aware of any surface and root issues that may be present. Has this person shown a history of reckless behavior and the lack of ability to learn from bad mistakes? Have you become a crutch to this person who sees you as a way to get bailed out of bad decisions? Pain can be a teacher and many times we as people learn better when pain is associated with a lesson. That's the reason why parents discipline their children! God says that even Jesus learned by suffering (Hebrews 5:8). We have to be aware of if we're truly helping someone, or just enabling their consistently bad behavior. When we enable a friend or family member to continue with irresponsible behavior we're no longer helping them. It's a huge commonly made mistake that people think they're showing love by giving, when in actuality they're hurting because the person isn't learning lessons of how to be better. We have to learn lessons and improve behavior in every aspect of our lives, but especially when dealing with others.

Let's reexamine our example about lending the light bill money to our loved one. Your decision on giving may hinge on the answers to those questions mentioned in the last paragraph. Maybe you say yes if they admit they made some poor financial choices, accept responsibility, and let you know they're trying to do better. But maybe you say no if they don't do those things. There could be several other factors besides what I mentioned that can affect the situation also. But the main point is to force ourselves to think through long term affects of decisions we make. Along with that, the other factor that's important is actually talking through those situations with the people involved. That feeling we have of loving someone and wanting to avoid tension or negativity can be dangerous if it influences us to not have conversations that'll encourage someone to improve their behavior. By not having tough conversations about appropriate situations we're hindering our growth as people. Communication is vital to not just romantic relationships but all relationships. It's easier to avoid conflict, but that certainly doesn't mean its best to avoid conflict. Often times the easier option turns out to be the less rewarding or beneficial option. We force ourselves and others to grow when we don't sugar coat things and paint a pretty picture all the time. Because of different personality types it matters how we have those tough conversations with each other. An ugly truth is better than a pretty lie. But that doesn't excuse us from still being tactful and careful with our words and how we use them within these conversations with others. In the gospels Jesus displays several examples of knowing how to interact with people and using the proper judgment of situations. We have to learn from His examples and replicate our decision making process after Christ's.

Forcing ourselves to be more aware of the long term affects of decisions is vital because that's what Christ did. By asking ourselves the questions of "Does this please God", "Does this help the other person get to heaven?", "Does this help me get to heaven?", we help ourselves to have eyes like Jesus. Seeing situations the way He did while He was on this earth will enhance our lives and the lives of those around us. Jesus wasn't the most popular person because of what He taught. Many people only went to Him to get healed or see some sign or miracle. Many interactions He had with the Pharisees, Scribes, and Chief Priests were filled with their deception and attempts to trick Him. He saw right through their futile attempts and always was able to give spiritual lessons and applications. We are capable of handling situations the same way Jesus did. We're capable of using self control to not respond to people negatively in situations where it may seem warranted. We're capable of recognizing someone not being genuine with us because He left us the examples in the scriptures as a guideline for us to follow. He told us several times in several ways to be like Him. He wouldn't set us up for failure, nor tell us to do something that we couldn't do. God created us and He's well aware of our capabilities. We're the ones that doubt and neglect our abilities to do things. We just have to make concerted efforts to be better. Far too many people that know about how Jesus handled situations so well just attribute it to Him being God on earth. They think that because He was God on earth He was able to display attributes that we as normal people can't. In terms of the miracles and certain teachings He did it's true we can't duplicate those. But to assume that all the traits He showed are above us is erroneous. Hebrews 4:15 mentions how Jesus was "in all points tempted as we are, yet without sin" and there's examples in the gospels where Jesus showed the same human emotions that we show like sorrow, compassion, joy, sadness, confusion and anger among many others. When the devil tempted Him in Matthew 4:1-11 its evident how Jesus succeeded over Him because He was so consistent with His responses. With every temptation Jesus answered the devil with "it is written". His strength was in the word of God. Even when the devil used a passage of scripture out of context, Jesus still responded with the word of God. The blueprint for us to follow is making sure our actions are guided by the word of God. So our goal is to train ourselves how to take the lessons we learn from the examples given in scripture and actually apply them to how we respond to situations in life.

Training ourselves to see situations as Jesus did is difficult but doable. We must make the diligent effort to searching for the deeper meaning of situations when things occur. By deeper meaning I'm referring to the spiritual application of the earthly situation that's happening. We must try to be aware of the eternal affects that earthly situations have on us and those around us. Jesus knew the importance of being spiritually minded instead of earthly minded and He taught that lesson to as many people as much as possible. Because He knew the importance of it, He gave the effort that was necessary for Him to give. We must understand that diligent effort is consistently giving your absolute best. It's not a half-hearted effort and it's not a strong effort given for a short period of time. It's giving 100% effort 100% of the time. Being able to give that effort with a spiritually focused mind is invaluable to us having discernment that will help us navigate through life. It's also another example of God commanding us to do something that is for our best interest. In Colossians 3:1-2 God's word tells us to "seek those things above" and "set your mind on things above". God tells us how to think because we can control our thoughts. We can't let ourselves be too simple. 1st Peter 5:8 tells us to "be sober and vigilant". Those words mean be clear-headed, restrained, alert, aware, watchful, observant, and attentive. We're spiritual beings that struggle to keep our perspective on life spiritually focused. When we're not short-sighted and we're focused on the spiritual things that are most important, we fulfill God's will for us. God has designed life in such a way that we are constantly introduced to things that we must learn and then do. The earthly situations are the only way for Him to teach us the spiritual lessons. So we have to be able to learn the spiritual lessons from earthly situations and then respond with actions that show we're spiritually focused. First we're introduced to and taught a topic. Then we must do our part to learn and understand the topic. Through various attempts and efforts we must get to the point where we understand the topic well enough to perform it correctly. Let's try to illustrate that process by relating it to a sporting contest and how coaches and players try to win a game.

The coaches know the strengths and weaknesses of their own team based on the time spent with them. So when getting ready for a game the coaches have to evaluate the strengths and weaknesses of the opponent.

Then based off that evaluation the coaches try to figure out ways to maximize their own team's strengths and minimize their weaknesses. They also try to figure out how to maximize the opponent's weaknesses and minimize the opponent's strengths. After studying those things the coaches devise a game plan and try to figure out how to execute the game plan based on those strengths and weaknesses. Recognizing those strengths and weaknesses of each side of the contest is one challenge. Devising a successful game plan of how to exploit those strengths and weaknesses is the next challenge. And then after those the greatest challenge is executing the game plan well. That's where the players come in. The coaches do their best to communicate the game plan to the players. The players understanding and executing the game plan is most vital. God is the coach and we are the players. He has evaluated the strengths and weaknesses of people, his players, as well as the opponent, the devil. The game plan He created is the Bible and He's done everything He can to effectively communicate to us how to execute His game plan so we can have victory.

I'm biased because I like sports but that's the way we need to approach our lives on earth. Live as if we are trying to execute the guaranteed winning game plan for our spiritual well being. In sports no matter what the contest or the players, there is no such thing as an absolute guaranteed winning game plan. But in life there is, and it's called the Bible. We have to execute the game plan correctly so we can win the game. But life is obviously not a game and eternity in heaven or hell is the ultimate win or loss. We are spiritual beings temporarily confined to a physical realm. God put us on this earth for us to decide where we will spend eternity. We get to choose heaven by faithfully loving and obeying God. Or we choose hell by not faithfully loving and obeying God. God has told us through His word that there will be a final battle between God and the devil at the end of times. God's side will win so we should choose to be on the winning side. Our choice to be on God's side is a day by day process. That day by day process of decision making is how much we are giving ourselves to faithfully loving and obeying God. We constantly make decisions that as a whole will collectively determine which side we are choosing. We're told in 2nd Corinthians 5:10 and in Ecclesiastes 12:14 that we're going to be held accountable to God for the things we've done whether good or bad. We are all in the middle of the battle between God and the devil. They both want us on their side. The things we go through in our lives are battles in the war. So when we know God's word and actually live it out in our lives, we are executing that winning game plan He gave us.

First we must understand our own strengths and weaknesses. This is self awareness and far too many people lose the battle right here. Our weaknesses are our fleshly minds that focus on earthly things in the here and now. Those earthly things are temporary pleasures of this life that don't affect our well being in the next life. Our strengths that we have are our love and obedience towards God. God's word makes many promises to us about how life will come at us. He makes sure we know that both good and bad things will happen but He gives us what we need to know to be prepared to handle them. The one being who created life gave us as people the information we need to successfully live life. Knowing our opponent is the next key. 1st John 2:15-17 is pretty much God giving us the devil's game plan. Specifically verse 16 mentions the lust of the flesh, the lust of the eyes and the pride of life. The devil uses those three things to influence us to disobey God. They may look different depending upon the person and the situation but they are the root issues of sin. Every sin and disobedience we as people commit will fall into at least one of those three areas. The sin is either something that we think feels good to us, looks good to us or makes us feel prideful by earthly or fleshly standards. Each of those things can be good in the right context but often times they are misplaced and the devil has been using them since the beginning of time. Genesis 3:1-6 tells us about the first sin with Adam and Eve, and all three of the root issues of sin are present. Verse 6 says "when the woman saw that the tree was good for food" (lust of the flesh), "it was pleasant to the eyes" (lust of the eyes), "and a tree desirable to make one wise" (pride of life). Thousands of years have passed and billions have walked this earth but those three things are still the devil's most successful ways of influencing us to disobey God.

As the players our responsibility is to make sure we understand the game plan the coaches created and to execute it during the game. That's where our consistent and diligent studying of God's word comes in to play. When we submit to that deep level of commitment, God gives us discernment to clearly understand His will in situations. After we've recognized the strengths and weaknesses of us and our opponent the devil, and we know what his game plan is, we're set up for victory. Our execution of God's game plan is us living out the Bible in our everyday lives. We have all the tools we need to succeed. Our effort level just has to keep growing. There are certain passages of scripture that are really simple and self explanatory. One of them is James 4:7 which says "submit to God, resist the devil, and he will flee from you". That reads as a step by step process that's easy to follow and see results. First we must submit to God. That means no part of us is held back from allowing God to work through us and use us for His glory. Submitting to God is obedience to His word and the commands that He's given us. Then after submitting to God we can resist the devil. If we attempt to resist the devil without submitting to God, we're set up for failure. We can't defeat the devil on our own, we need God's help. God gives us the strength we need to resist the devil and his temptations of sin. After our resisting him, he flees. The devil knows he can't defeat God. So when we have God's strength with us by submitting and obeying God the devil will flee from us. What the verse doesn't say is that the devil won't come back. But we can know for sure from other passages of scripture with examples from people's lives in the Bible that the devil does come back. He comes back consistently to us when we don't have the strength of God. He is opportunistic and will offer us the temptations while we are weak. So that's why our execution of God's game plan is so important. The devil won't quit trying to get us to fall away from God. So that's why we can't quit and slack up on our efforts of staying close to God. The next verse James 4:8 says "draw near to God and He will draw near to you". That's just another reminder that our effort has to be there. God has equipped us with what we need to succeed we just have to realize the urgency, zeal, passion, fire and diligence that needs to be included in our efforts. When we keep giving God the efforts, He gives us the discernment. When we have the discernment and use it correctly we'll understand the difference between surface issues and root issues. When we understand those differences we're equipped to handle them better.

FIVE

THE RED LIGHT TEST

W hether we realize it or not, we pick and choose which areas of our lives we're going to control ourselves. We make those decisions based on what we value or what's most important to us. Being cognitive of our own selective behavior is an important step to enhancing our relationship with God and our overall quality of life. Controlling ourselves in difficult times is a test that we fail far too often. We have the ability to control ourselves but we minimize that ability by not using it effectively. Our ability to control our actions on a constant basis is dependent on the value that we place in the consequences or benefits that will result from those actions. Think about it in terms of what I like to call the "Red Light Test". As a matter of practice or habit when approaching a red light we make sure we stop for various reasons. Obeying the law, our physical safety and the well-being of others are the main reasons for stopping. The consequences of running the red light, such as getting a ticket or getting in a wreck, outweigh the benefits of running the light. The benefits may be getting to a destination faster or just having the satisfaction of beating the light. Because of all those variable outcomes, we made the conscious decision to not run red lights on a consistent basis. This is just one application of a concept that we use all the time, perhaps without realizing it. We constantly weigh the negative consequences versus the positive benefits of an action before doing or not doing it. Generally if the consequences outweigh the benefits we won't do the particular action. But when the benefits outweigh the consequences then we perform the action. We do this fairly often concerning earthly situations, either consciously or subconsciously. But imagine having that mindset with our relationship with God. Before we decide to do something we should compare the spiritual benefits versus the spiritual consequences.

Let's consider a situation where a married person has the opportunity to commit adultery. Say a married man and an unmarried female co-worker are attracted to each other. Often times this exact situation influences marital infidelity because the time, emotions and shared experiences in the workplace can feel very similar to a romantic relationship. For the sake of our example let's say both parties feel a mutual attraction. Then after some time passes the female worker makes evident signs that she is interested in something more. While she is dropping hints some thoughts can run through the man's mind. He starts to weigh what he sees as the consequences versus the benefits. He might think about the pain this will cause his spouse or that his spouse won't find out about it. He also may think about the physical and emotional pleasures he'll have. So he's constantly weighing the benefits versus the consequences until he makes his decision. But the issue is those are just the earthly ramifications of that situation. Where people get in trouble is being too short-sighted to weigh the spiritual consequences versus benefits. The spiritual consequences of adultery are extensive. The disobedience to several of God's commands are involved including not committing adultery, (Romans 13:9) loving your spouse, (Ephesians 5:25) resisting temptation, (James 1:12) fleeing sexual immorality (1st Corinthians 6:18) and many more that can apply (1st Peter 3:8, 1st Corinthians 7:9, 1st Timothy 4:12). The effect this has on God is that it disappoints, saddens and angers Him. (Romans 1:18, Genesis 6:5-6) Adultery is a very involved and deliberate sin because there are several thoughts and actions that lead up to the actual sinful act. Because of that there are various points where both parties have several opportunities to not go through with the sinful act. Obviously that example isn't relatable to everyone but the principle is the same. Many sins and temptations in life are gradual and we have ample opportunities to avoid or overcome them. We're told in 1st Corinthians 10:13 that we can escape from those temptations. God wouldn't tell us that if it wasn't true because it's impossible for Him to lie. (Titus 1:2) God has given us the strength and ability but we have to have the will and desire to follow through.

The key to understanding this concept is recognizing that whether consciously or subconsciously we put different levels of importance on everything. A common issue is that far too many people put the wrong level of importance on the wrong things. Whether that means putting a higher level of importance on something insignificant or putting a lower level of importance on something significant. Determining what levels of importance to put on things is dependent upon the value we see in certain things versus another. Some people value being a law abiding citizen. Because of that they curve their behavior in such a way as to avoid committing crimes. The respect and fear they have for laws and the punishments that are contained for breaking laws creates a high level of value. Since that has a high level of value it will take precedence over something else that doesn't have as much value. So when faced with a decision between those two, the one with the higher level of value placed on it will prevail. We have to correctly understand the correlation of physical laws and spiritual laws. Genesis 39:7-12 contains one of the more fascinating stories in all of scripture and it's a great example of how to deal with sexual temptation. A teenager named Joseph was being sexually pursued by his master's wife. His master Potiphar was a guard of the Egyptian ruler Pharaoh so it's probably safe to assume this woman was very attractive. She came on to him consistently and he denied her. It got to the point that he actually ran away to avoid sleeping with her. I was a teenage boy once and I know teenage boys place a good amount of value on the opposite sex. So it's amazing to see this story about how he was able to have the will power to resist her consistently. According to verses 8-9

Joseph apparently put way more value in obeying God and keeping the trust of Potiphar. He didn't mention punishment or consequences that would've risen from the situation had he chosen to give in to her. He showed a great deal of integrity because of where he placed his value. And because he valued obeying God, his behavior was consistent with that even in a difficult test.

When we compare two things that we value we can accurately see which is more important. Often times the only way for us to recognize what we value most is when we have to compare that thing to something else we also value. In Matthew 10:17-22 the story of the rich young ruler shows us this. He takes the initiative and runs up to Jesus to ask him how to receive eternal life. And then he shows that he's been obedient to God's word since he was a young boy. So up to this point in verse 20 he seems like he puts his value in the correct places such as spiritual matters. But then the young man was faced with a decision of what he valued the most. Spiritual things such as following Jesus, or physical things like his great possessions. He clearly chooses the physical things because he walked away from Jesus. It's interesting that the text says he was sad when hearing Jesus' answer and he walked away grieved. He was sad and grieved but not affected enough to actually change and make the right decision to follow Christ. Clearly the young man knew he valued his great possessions as well as spiritual matters and obeying God. But perhaps he never forced himself to compare the two in order to see which he valued more. He most likely never saw it as an issue that needed to be compared and never thought he'd have to choose between the two. He was either unaware of or didn't properly apply Christ's teaching from the Sermon on the Mount in Matthew 6:24. It says "No one can serve two masters; for either he will hate the one and love the other, or else he will be loyal to the one and despise the other. You cannot serve God and riches." I'm obviously just speculating because scripture doesn't give us any more information about this man. But what is clear from what we can see is that he valued both spiritual matters and earthly possessions. And when faced with the decision between the two, he chose the wrong option. Whether it was the first time in his life that he had to choose or not, doesn't really matter. What does matter is that we see this example and learn from it for our lives. We must be aware enough to notice when we're faced with having to choose what's more important between spiritual matters and anything else. Then after noticing, we must make the proper decision to choose the spiritual over the physical by placing the most value in the spiritual.

It's easy to look at the rich young ruler's situation and pick it apart. We can point out the flaws that this young man had and chastise him for making the wrong decision. But events like that are contained in scripture because we need to learn from the mistakes of others so we don't make the same ones. We're all faced with the exact same situation every single day. We are constantly choosing whether we value spiritual things more or earthly things more. The decision just manifests itself in various ways. But we each have to make the decision of picking which is more important between spiritual things or physical things. It's not a one-time decision; we have to keep making that decision no matter how many times we're faced with it. While it may not be as obvious as the rich young ruler's situation we have it the same. By not being aware of it or diminishing the importance of it we are actually endangering our eternal well being. We have to keep learning how to put the right levels of importance in the appropriate areas of life. Because we're all so different, some people are naturally more self aware than others. While understanding this and carrying it out may be more difficult for some than others, we still have the responsibility to do it. It's literally a matter of spiritual life or death. And that's the one decision we can't get wrong. We have to remember that whatever level of effort that's required to be put forth is worth it. We have to make sure we put the right level of value on the most important components of life. Those should be our spiritual well being comprised of our faithful love and obedience to God's word. When we do that, our behavior will be consistent and we'll exercise good habits. Those good habits will become our manner of life and make up who we are at our very core.

SIX

THE HEART OF
THE MATTER

Self awareness is one of the essential details to life. Being constantly in tune with the health of our thoughts, words, deeds and desires is critical to navigating through life. We have to learn what we're vulnerable to and work towards getting better. Sometimes that means facing the situation and other times that means avoiding the situation. Before I was married I really struggled with watching inappropriate content on the internet. I knew it was wrong and I really didn't want to keep doing what was wrong. But often times my weaknesses would give in to my desires. I struggled with this for years but through the grace and power of God I finally was able to overcome this struggle. While being married helped, the biggest reason I was able to overcome was because I made the choice to let God work in me. My heart and mind were completely made up that I was going to do my best to do what's right in every situation in life and this happened to be one of them. Obviously I don't always succeed, but I try to stay aware and keep trying to do what's right. The way I was able to do it was to avoid the temptations. When I got the urges to look at things I shouldn't, I'd do various things to help calm the urge. I was able to focus on God's will for me which was and always is to faithfully love and obey Him. Focusing on His will changed my disobedient desires into obedient ones. This is what is meant by Psalm 37:4 that says "delight yourself in the Lord and He will give you the desires of your heart". By focusing on His will I delighted myself in the Lord. I changed so much until I started taking pleasure and enjoying showing my love for God by obeying Him. Since I took pleasure in obeying Him my desires went from doing what I wanted to do, to doing what He wanted me to do. So when the verse promises that God would give the desires of my heart it proved true. But the key is my desires changed to match His desires. He gave me the desires of my heart after they changed to match His. In chapter four, I detailed the differences between surface issues and root issues. The ultimate root issue in life that spreads across so many areas is our heart problem.

Many people don't really understand what is meant when discussing their heart. People frequently use the phrase "I've made my mind up" but your mind and your heart aren't the same. Your mind is a part of your heart, but it's not the summation. Thoughts can come into our minds without us purposely putting them there. I can be carrying on a conversation with my wife and out of nowhere, for no reason and completely unrelated to what we were talking about, I start thinking about the video to "Thriller" from Michael Jackson. There are also the times songs we don't even like or haven't heard that much get stuck in our heads and we randomly sing the lyrics. As with many of my examples that I use, they may be silly, but hopefully they're driving home the point. Your mind isn't your heart because there are plenty of times that you think things you don't want to. Likewise your actions aren't your heart because sometimes you do things you don't want to. Your feelings aren't your heart because sometimes you feel a certain way you don't want to. God tells us what kind of heart He's pleased with so we don't have to guess (Matthew 5:8 & 1ˢᵗ timothy 1:5). Your heart is your core or center of who you are. It's a combination of those different parts of you at different times. It's the combination of your thoughts, feelings, desires, words, actions and more. It's who or what you're known as, your character, your truth, your whole being. Most importantly we're in control of who we are and the condition of our heart.

There are two nearly identical situations that I will attempt to use to explain why the condition of your heart is so important. In Luke 1:11-17 the angel Gabriel prophesied to Zacharias of the son that he and his wife Elizabeth would have. Zacharias and his wife were both old and this was a shock to him. In verse 18 Zacharias questions Gabriel about the validity of his claim. Because of the doubt Zacharias showed his punishment was that he would be unable to speak until the child is born.

Then further on in the same chapter we see almost the same thing happen to the Mary. In verses 28-33 is where Gabriel tells Mary about the child she'll have. Verse 34 Mary questions Gabriel very similarly to how Zacharias did. Go ahead and read verses 18 and 34 and see if there's a difference. They both gave what seemed to be logical reasons, age and virginity respectively, for why they hesitated to fully believe what Gabriel told them. Both of their questions made perfect sense and seemed to be very valid from a logical perspective. However they were different because what Gabriel told them afterwards was different. He told Zacharias that he would be mute because of his doubt, but Mary gets further explanation in verses 35-37. So in verse 38 she verbalizes her belief. There's no way to know if there was more of an exchange between Gabriel and Zacharias so I can only go off what we see in the text and I don't want to add more than what's included. So as far as we know Zacharias never verbalized his belief nor do we know if Mary was persuaded by what Gabriel said in verses 35-37. Whether or not Mary already believed what Gabriel told her before he gave her the explanation we'll never know. Although there are things we can't know, we can learn an important lesson from what we can see. These situations started off the same but the difference is that God knows the heart. That's a very familiar phrase many people have heard and used. But what it means is that as our Creator and Father He sees things we as people can't see. In 1st Samuel 16 God chose young David to be the next king of Israel while others wanted to choose one of David's brothers based off appearance. In verse 7 God says that "man looks at the outward appearance, but the LORD looks at the heart". God knowing the hearts of His people He created means He knows how we are going to handle situations. We as people can look at the similarities of Zacharias and Mary's responses see the differences in the results and it can make us wonder why he got punished but she didn't? Those things we don't know don't matter because their hearts were shown. If Zacharias had a heart to believe he would have believed. Likewise if Mary didn't have a heart to believe it wouldn't matter how much persuading Gabriel did.

When our hearts aren't right that can lead to problems of us disturbing and perverting things that shouldn't be. When our hearts aren't right our motives and reasons for doing things have selfish origins. It also can cause us to deflect blame and not accept responsibility for things we do and say. If we're not careful those things can become part of our character. We can't ignore the compounding affects things have on us. One thing leads to another and before we recognize it, we're too late. These types of things can create cognitive dissonance. Which is a fancy term for saying someone's thoughts, attitudes, and behaviors are unstable. You ever know someone who is "wishy washy", just not really firm or decisive about much of anything. Our lives need to reflect the guidance and direction that God gives us in His word. It's ok to be unsure of your direction in certain instances for certain periods of time. When we are consistently indecisive that's an issue that needs to be resolved immediately. As a child of God we all have the same direction, which is heaven. God put us on this earth for us to choose where we will spend eternity. He has created things that scream evidence of Him as creator. He has given us every reason to love Him. He has told us the blessings that are prepared for us obeying Him and the punishments prepared for those who disobey Him. There are ample blessings in this life and the next. He has also told us about the consequences for disobedience in this life and the next. So we have to be intentional about our direction in life and about our actions being in unison with that direction. Being intentional about those things is how we change our hearts. Changing our heart is one of the definitions of repentance. It also carries with it the idea of remorse and or admission of guilt. Thinking or feeling differently because of the guilt and a reversal of a decision. All of those things are a part of repentance and they show that we have control of our heart's condition.

Since changing our heart is so difficult we have to get to the point where we're humble enough to admit that what we want doesn't matter. First, we can all determine the foundation that Jesus is God and human. So part of Him is from His Heavenly Father, and the other part of Him is from His earthly mother. While in the garden of Gethsemane, He was under extreme stress and worry because of the punishment that lay ahead of Him. The physical part of Him wanted nothing to do with the extreme physical pain He was about to endure. However, don't forget that the Old Testament gives the message that the Savior will have to die for the sins of the world. So the spiritual part of Him couldn't wait to die for our sins. That part of Him was eager to endure the suffering just to show us the EXTENT of His love for us. While in

Gethsemane he prayed three times "Father, if it is Your will, take this cup away from Me; nevertheless not My will, but Yours, be done" (Matthew 26:42-44 and Mark 14:41). So here is Jesus Christ the Son of GOD praying to His Father to let him be spared from the suffering! He humbled himself and acknowledged that what he wanted didn't matter. This is the only perfect man that has ever, or will ever live. Think about that for a second, just one man out of the billions of people throughout the history of the world lived perfect in God's sight. If there is any person who you might think deserves to get what he wants, wouldn't it be the only perfect person in the history of the world past, present, or future. Of course it would be. But not even He got what He wanted all the time. We all need to be humble enough to take the lesson from this story that what we want doesn't matter. Since we all have sinned and fallen short of the glory of God (Romans 3:23), we need to constantly and continuously put ourselves in our rightful place, which is behind God (Luke 14:11). If you think about it, it makes perfect sense. God has infinite wisdom, so shouldn't we trust in the one who knows more than we will ever know. Shouldn't we follow the commands and the desire of the one who spoke the universe into existence (Genesis 1:3)? Of course we should. This example from the garden of Gethsemane is a great foundation to start at while trying to be like Christ. We will face situations in life that we think we know what's best for us, but if we take the example from Christ, we will be blessed. Jesus trusted and obeyed, so we need to do the same. That will help us change our heart.

SEVEN

FOCUS & PATIENCE

Patience is dependent on focus. Our ability to wait on something is related to how focused we are on it. Our minds are very powerful and we often don't recognize the power we have. By not controlling what we dwell on, we're letting our mind control us instead of us controlling our mind. When we're waiting on a situation to develop or turn out a certain way we can become impatient when we think about it too much. Whereas if we would control our thoughts and not think about the situation so much we'd be less anxious about the outcome. Often times when we're not focused on something it tends to happen sooner. Or it might not happen sooner, but we'll be more at peace while waiting for the situation to unfold. When we're in a situation that we can't control and we have to just wait for something to happen it can have many different affects on us. It can be frustrating, depressing, confusing, humbling and many other things. We're the ones who decide how a situation is going to affect us. Philippians 4:8 gives us a guide on how we should focus our thoughts. It tells us what to think on by using several positive descriptive words. If we pay attention to the fact that this verse is a direct command from God it carries more weight to it. Most people easily identify with commands that start with either "thou shall" or "thou shall not". For some reason though far too many people struggle to recognize that God instructs us to do or not do plenty of other things without using those specific phrases. The verse in Philippians 4:8 is no different and carries no less weight than the command to not kill. Understanding scriptural authority in that manner helps us to know how serious God is with everything He tells us. We shouldn't keep giving away the power our minds have by neglecting to use that power properly. We need to take God's word serious enough to learn how to focus on what He wants.

I had an epiphany about how being focused can affect our behavior and awareness years ago while I was in the grocery store. I went in the store with four items I wanted to get. I can't remember what the actual items were but that's irrelevant. I didn't write the list down nor did I put it in my phone so I just recited the four items in my head in the same order. I went up and down each aisle scanning the shelves for the items I needed. I didn't do it purposely but I found each item in the exact order as I was reciting them. What made this event stand out to me even years later is that three of the items were on the same aisle. However I hadn't noticed the other items because I was so focused on each item one at a time.

That experience may not impress you but it fascinates me. My focus was so intense that I found the items in the exact order I was saying them. That encouraged me to understand that if I put my mind to something, I can achieve it. The other piece of my amazement with this situation is that when I focused on one thing, I blocked out other things, even things that were also important to me. Each item on the list was important, but as I was focused on the 1st one, I blocked out the other three. Then when I got the 2nd one I blocked out the remaining two items and so on. If I was able to have that focus on something as simple as a grocery list, I should be able to have that focus on more important parts of life.

The amount of focus we put on something and the patience we display while enduring the situation can and will affect our actions. We can learn from Peter when Jesus and the disciples were in the garden of Gethsemane the night of Christ's betrayal in Luke 22:47-51. After Judas kissed Jesus the disciples asked "Shall we strike with the sword?" Without waiting for Jesus to answer Peter cut off the ear of Malchus, who was the high priest's servant. But Jesus was displeased with this and not only did He rebuke Peter's action but He also healed Malchus' ear. This event is such a blatant lesson on patience. We have to apply this lesson to our lives. Wait on God to answer us before doing what we think is best. When we're praying about a situation and waiting for an answer it's tough to be patient. We want our answer so bad that often times we will force what we can so it will turn out in our favor. But we're limited because we make those decisions based off what we want. So when we're praying for something and we have to wait on the answer from God we have to not act rashly so we don't cut off someone's ear, figuratively speaking. During that event in Gethsemane Peter was focused on not letting anything happen to Jesus. He was so focused on what he wanted that he ignored what Jesus wanted. How often do you do that in your life? I definitely know I'm guilty of that. Peter's mental focus was a determining factor in his actions. We're the same so we have to be aware of it.

Several times in scripture God describes that we should be eagerly waiting for heaven. (1st Cor 1:7, Phil 3:20, Heb 9:28) He also tells us to focus our minds on heaven (Col 3:1-2 & Rom 12:1-2). Those two things go hand in hand so it's not an accident that He tells us to do both multiple times. Heaven is better than anything this earth has to offer. God never tells us to do something that will make us worse off than what we were before. He always wants us to improve as His children. Focusing our hearts and minds on heaven is just another example of God telling us to do something that is for our benefit. If we're seriously focused on heaven we'll think about it frequently. We'll think about how it's going to be once we're there and what we have to do to get there. Focusing on it will make us eager and willing to go. Being eager to go to heaven will influence our actions so that we do what God says is necessary to get there. That will also give us a great perspective on life because we'll know what really matters. We won't be so negatively affected by events in this life because we'll know what's waiting for us in the next life. If someone loses all their material possessions but they are focused on heaven, they'll know those things can be replaced. When you're focused on heaven, your identity won't be in things of this world. When you have a loved one who loses their life, focusing on heaven will help you remember that one day you're going to lose your life also. Focusing on heaven can help us get through any other challenging situation.

Focusing on going through something can seem like time goes by slow. Because focusing on going through something involves thinking about what's unpleasant about the experience and the weaknesses that's causing the struggle. Focusing on getting to something like an end result or destination can seem to help time go by fast. That's because we're more looking past the obstacles and the destination has more value than the journey. Having that mindset is in conjunction with Romans 8:18 that says "For I consider that the sufferings of this present time are not worthy to be compared with the glory which shall be revealed in us". That means that looking towards the prize in the future is better than looking at the obstacles that face us in the present. The book of Philippians was written by Paul while he was in prison in Rome. Paul could've focused on how miserable it was to be chained to a Roman guard all day or the poor conditions of the holding area he was confined to. But instead the premise of the letter is telling the Christians there in Philippi to have joy. Some variation of the words joy and rejoice are mentioned several times throughout the letter. The 1st portion of chapter two exhorts us to have the mind of Christ. The theme of the letter can be summed up by the phrase if your mind is set on Christ you'll have joy. Being in prison didn't steal Paul's joy. James 1:2 tells us to "count it all joy" when we endure trials. When events occur in our life we have to use them for our growth because that's why God allows us to go through those things. Whether it's something positive or negative we need to understand that God wants us to grow closer to Him. In Acts 5:41 Peter and the apostles rejoiced after they were beaten for proclaiming Christ. These examples are contained in scripture for us to know that we too can be so focused on heaven that the affairs of this life won't have such profound affects on us.

EIGHT

NO EXCUSES FAITH

Faith can't be summed up by just thinking positively, however that is an aspect of it. We must first have the positive thinking to believe that we can accomplish a task. Believing that we can accomplish the task is essential, because if we don't believe then we won't perform any actions. While in tough situations we need to see the value in positive thinking and choose to give strong, consistent effort to doing it. But it's hard to force ourselves to be positive when the situation we're going through is difficult. The easy thing to do is give ourselves an excuse as to why we're not being positive. We use excuses as an easy way of rationalizing to ourselves why we're giving up. We face what we perceive as too much resistance and we give up. But positive thinking is just the first aspect of doing something. Would someone do something if they were convinced they will fail? Would someone make the efforts to start their own business if they knew that they'd be wasting time, money and resources? Many people will stress the fact that we as people have different personalities and that some people will naturally have it easier to be positive. That is true, but that's not a reason to not try. If something is harder for you to do should you just give up and not try? Of course not because if something is hard we should believe we can overcome it. So while positive thinking is just one part of what faith is, it's important to be able to understand the relationship. Our faith can't be in ourselves, it should be in God. So instead of doubting if we're able to accomplish a task, we should have faith in God accomplishing the task through us or by using us. That's the difference between faith and positive thinking. Who or what is the basis for our belief will determine how we respond or react to various situations.

One day I was talking to a father who has two daughters. He explained to me the differences between them in terms of academics. The older daughter found academics naturally tougher and the younger one found them easier. The younger daughter wouldn't have to study hard to retain information so she was usually more prepared for tests and performed better. The older daughter struggled to get good grades consistently. Despite the natural differences in the two daughters he expected A's from both of them. The younger daughter could study one hour and make an A on a test, while the older daughter would have to study two hours to make an A on the same test material. They both had to do what was necessary for them to do in order to make A's. However it looked differently in both of their lives.

The older daughter could've just studied one hour and been content with less of a grade, but she chose not to. She chose to do whatever it took in order for her to be prepared enough to make an A. Her choice to study more was grounded in the fact that she believed that if she studied longer it would actually help. If she thought that she couldn't retain the test material no matter how many hours she studied that would have hindered her desire to put in the effort to studying. They each should do their part to study to retain the knowledge they need, but with the faith and trust of God's ability and willingness to help them retain the knowledge successfully. All the studying in the world won't help if God doesn't allow us to retain the information we studied. Can we recognize those types of situations in our relationship with God? Do we make excuses why we don't put forth the requisite effort to do God's will in our lives? How many times do we choose not to talk to someone about giving their life to Christ because we convince ourselves they're not interested? How many blessings in our lives do we block because we make excuses why we don't do our part to receive them?

In Philippians 1:3-6 Paul is showing his appreciation at the participation the people in Philippi had with working to spread the gospel. Paul commends them but within the compliment of them, he gives glory and honor to the one it is really due to. He says in verse six that "He who has begun a good work in you will complete it until the day of Jesus Christ." He points the focus to God being the one that is working through the people in Philippi. So while Paul is complimenting them, he's really complimenting God because he recognizes that God is using them. He is also reminding them that God is using them. By doing this, Paul is attempting to make sure they don't get prideful or haughty into thinking that they're so great. We can't think of ourselves as having such great ability, we must humbly recognize that God gives us the ability and that He does the work. If God didn't give us the ability, we couldn't do the work no matter how hard we try. The only thing we do is be submissive to God's will and allow Him to work through us. As children of God, we have to make the choice to allow God to work through us to accomplish His will. We can be confident that God began the work and He'll complete the work. While the specific context of the passage is talking about spreading the gospel, the learning principle that's prevalent is that God works through us. Our faith will strengthen the more we understand that we don't have to solely depend on our own limited capabilities but that we can depend on God's unlimited capabilities. Since we can trust in God who has unlimited capabilities, what room do we have for excuses as to why we can't do something or accomplish a certain task? If that thing or task is something that pleases God or assists us in honoring God, where is the room for us to not give our best efforts to do our part? 2nd Timothy 2:13 mentions that "when we are faithless, He remains faithful." God always does His part He's just waiting on us to fulfill our end of the deal.

We have to choose to do what God wants us to do for us to succeed in life situations. In chapter four I detailed how important it is for our actions to be in line with what God's word says. So in doing what His word says, we also accept that we get what His words says will be the result of us obeying Him. It will look differently depending on the situation and the person but there is one huge commonality present no matter what. The choice we make when we realize how hard something is going to be is whether or not we choose to give more effort or less effort. Let me put it to you in numerical terms. Let's say I'm faced with a task and before starting it I decide I will give 80% effort. But then after I start the task I realize it will take 100% effort in order for me to complete it successfully. The critical point is when I realize the task is going to take more effort than I was initially willing to give. It's at that time I must decide if I'm going to give that extra effort or not. And if I choose not to, I can make an excuse for not giving the extra effort. The excuse can help me feel better about not giving more effort. It's easy to see the obstacle and how it will stop you. But is much more difficult to see how the obstacle won't stop you. It's more difficult, but it's also more rewarding when you overcome it. We have to be uncomfortable with making excuses for ourselves. Many of us make excuses for why we won't do something, but then pray and ask God to do it for us. It's like we try to use God for what we want instead of letting God use us for what He wants. James 2:14-26 shows how understanding the relationship between faith and actions is so vital. To sum it all up verse 22 says "Do you see that faith was working together with his works, and by works faith was made perfect?" Depending upon which Bible translation you have the words works and actions are used interchangeably. And the word perfect in this usage means complete. You may be familiar with the old sayings of "putting feet to your prayers" or that "God helps those who help themselves". Those phrases aren't found in scripture but the principles and lessons contained in each of the sayings are true. You must do your part for your prayers to be answered. That's not a guarantee of getting yes for an answer but it will help us recognize our answer better. If we've done everything in our power, either one of the things we tried will work and that'll be our yes or none of the things we tried will work and that'll be our no. Sometimes something unexpected will happen that'll answer the prayer. We may be in the midst of trying things to resolve the situation when something unexpected happens to resolve the situation. Scripture is filled with examples of God wanting people to do something so that He can accomplish something through them that'll give Him glory. One such example is in Joshua chapter 6 when Joshua and the people of Israel circled the city of Jericho for six days and then the walls came down on the seventh after the great shout. God planned that and commanded them to do that so He could get the glory out of how He blessed them. God getting glory is His will because He wants us to recognize His greatness and how much He loves us. In this situation God promised the nation of Israel a great land flowing with milk and honey. He is always trying to get us to appreciate how much He loves us to the point where we have enough gratitude and allegiance towards Him that causes us to obey Him.

Another result God wants from how well He blesses

us is that other people can be affected as well. One of the reasons we were put on this earth is to impact other people. That's why after God made Adam He said "it's not good for man to be alone. I will make a helper comparable to him" (Genesis 2:18). He designed the church to be a group of believers united together with the same heart and mind (Acts 4:32). No matter what the situation or activity no one can do everything by themselves. We all need help. We have to be intentional in helping others in this life. When someone who doesn't have a relationship with God sees how God blesses people who follow Him, it can influence them to want to learn more about how they can live the same type of life. We see this obvious example in Joshua chapter 2 with Rahab the harlot and the Israelite spies. Other nations of people heard about the good ways that God blessed the people of Israel. Rahab actually did something drastic to show that she believed in the power of God. From what she heard about the nation of Israel and their triumphs she knew it was God helping them. Because of that she made sure to align herself with them in any way she could. This was the exact outcome God wanted for that situation. The people of Israel took the city Jericho and Rahab and her family were spared because of their belief in God. God wants to use each of us for situations like that. He wants us to give Him glory with our lives so then others can see our example and give Him glory with their lives. Depending on the situation reasons and excuses can be a matter of opinion and perspective. Normally the person giving the excuse sees it as a reason and the person receiving the reason sees it as an excuse. But in our relationship with God there are no valid reasons for not living for Him by loving faithful obedience.

Following Christ has to be important enough to us so that we won't even desire to give excuses of why we won't follow Him. There are multiple accounts in the gospels (Matt 9:27-31, Luke 18:35-43 & Matthew 20:29-34) about blind men not allowing their blindness to hinder their attempts to get to Jesus. Matthew 9:20-22 & Luke 8:43-48 gives the account of a woman with a flow of blood for 12 years. Even though her condition got worse because no doctor could help her, her faith was so strong that she believed Jesus could heal her without even getting His attention. She just wanted to touch the bottom of his clothes to get healed. In Matthew 15:21-28 the Canaanite woman was very determined despite the fact that she wasn't a Jew so she was deterred by Jesus and His disciples. But her daughter's health was too important for her to take no for an answer since she knew that Jesus was able to heal. Even after Jesus called her a dog, she didn't respond negatively but rather continued to stay focused on doing what she could to have her daughter healed. Verse 27 shows that she knew His power and capability was vast enough to help her. She even displayed humility by agreeing with her being a dog. Jesus then commends her response and pays off her persistence by healing her daughter. She had several opportunities to not have faith in Jesus healing her daughter but she refused to give up. Our faith can be that strong and we can be that determined to believe that Christ will do great things for us if we let Him.

Exodus 4:10-16 gives us a great example of how

powerful faith is. Faith is so dangerous and powerful that we can actually use it to the negative if we're not careful. Often times our negative faith is greater than our positive faith. In chapter three of Exodus God tells Moses that He will use him to get Pharaoh to release the people of Israel. In verses 10-15 God and Moses have a back and forth with Moses giving God multiple excuses as to why he shouldn't be the one to go to Pharaoh. Then in the first nine verses of chapter four God gives Moses three signs to perform that will prove that God is with Moses in front of Pharaoh. But in verse 10 Moses gives his final excuse. Moses had the wrong kind of faith in that he couldn't speak well enough to lead the Jews from Egypt. We must be careful with our faith because of how powerful faith is. Moses gives us the example of how even when we use our faith for the negative, it can still come to fruition. Moses was so convinced that he couldn't speak for God that God finally said He would use Aaron to speak. What Moses missed was that God was trying to teach him that He can do anything. God didn't pick Moses because he could speak well, God chose Moses because he couldn't speak well. His strength is made perfect in weakness (2nd Corinthians 12:9). This is one of many examples in scripture of God using someone with a deficiency in a certain area to do something great. That causes the person as well as others to know that God must've been the one to accomplish the feat as opposed to the individual. We won't always know what God is up to but we can make sure we trust that it's best for us.

NINE

FINISH LINE

Our lives are telling a story and we're writing a new chapter each day. The more aware we are of what we're writing, the better the content will be. The less aware of what we're writing, the worse the content will be. Life offers us many diverse avenues of what we can spend our thoughts, time, effort and attention to. We can't just go along with the flow and not focus on what's most important. The big picture of our life is made up of the little picture. If I wrote this book without being aware of how or what I was writing it wouldn't make any sense. (I'm assuming this book made sense.) What if I wasn't paying attention to the structure of what I was writing? And what if the chapters didn't relate to each other at all? The words compile to create sentences, which make the paragraphs that become the chapters. What if I combined random chapters together that each talked about completely different ideas. There'd be no kind of flow or ultimate point to get from the content. (I'm assuming I properly communicated a flow to the content of this book.) My goal is that we understand how to handle our relationships with God better by focusing on four things. It all starts with studying God's word on a consistent basis because that's how He speaks to us. Then we must improve our self awareness of what's going on in our life in comparison to God's word. After recognizing what's going on we have to make the right choice to obey what God says from His word. Finally after making the choice to obey God we must have the self control to actually do it consistently.

We all have lives that include challenges. Some challenges affect some people more than others. Ten people can face the exact same issue and handle it in ten different ways. God created us all differently so He knows how to handle us. Because of those differences it's not good for us to compare our lives to the lives of others. There are so many different variables that go into each of our lives that we can't accurately compare. It's hard enough for us to understand the path that God has for our own lives, much less trying to figure out the path He has for someone else's. Many people look at the lives of celebrities and desire to have the fame and or riches that they see. But so many celebrities are prisoners to their own fame and they're miserable. As for the money there's only but so much you can have before you become bored with accumulating things. We can't get so caught up with what other people have and what we don't have because everything isn't for everybody. In Matthew 6 Jesus mentions how the Pharisees fast and pray for the approval of men instead of God. He says that surely they have their reward meaning the approval of men

Even within our own lives there are too many variables to consider that would completely change who we are. Certain events can happen to us at certain times that will affect us way differently had that same event happened at another time. My parents divorced when I was nine years old. I would've been a completely different person had they stayed together or divorced once I was already an adult. I've had a few near death experiences at different times in my life. Had those happened earlier I wouldn't have been mature enough to learn from them and change the way I did. Had my wife and I met each other ten years prior to when we first met, we wouldn't have gotten married. We each were completely different people than who we each matured to be by time we met. From the schools we attend to the jobs we work to which checkout line we choose at the grocery store. Any particular instance can completely change our lives. It's all about how aware we are of our lives and what we're learning through the situations. God allows us to go through things for us to learn how to live better for Him. What do you expect from God and how do you view Him? Is He just a parachute that we use when we need Him or just in case of emergency? Or is He the pilot who we trust to fly the plane as we are the passengers? Do we expect Him to just fulfill our requests like a magic genie? Or do we understand that we serve Him and not the other way around?

Your view of God must start with understanding that He is the Creator of all things, the Supreme being, the One True God and besides Him there is no other. Because of His abundant love toward us He gives us life on earth and provides us with a perfect guidebook for how to live right. He wants us to understand the correlations between the physical matters of this life and how they affect our spiritual well being in this life and the next. As we go through life we're going to face situations that we'll need to make decisions on how to handle them. God's word is filled with not just commands from Him, but lessons from the lives of others. With the events in scripture being thousands of years old we have the benefit of hindsight to know what were the proper decisions made. We need to learn the lessons from the examples in scripture in order to make better decisions with our current life situations. The more we know and understand about God's will through His word, the clearer it'll be to discern the situations we're going through. We must also learn to have a pure heart that puts the proper amount of value and importance on the things that God does. As we continue to grow closer to Him we must be focused enough on our levels of humility and self control to carry out His will for us. His will is always going to be for us to faithfully love and obey Him by His word. When we focus enough on Him then the things of this world will become less important to us. And if worldly things aren't as important to us as spiritual things then we won't make excuses for ourselves for choosing them. All of the areas of our life can be used to glorify God. Through all the triumphs, trials, successes, pain or perseverance we have to keep choosing God. Over and over again, day after day, month after month, year after year, no matter the situation, keep choosing God. The hard times are supposed to be hard because God told us they would be. He promised us that He would help us overcome this world and guide us through it. We just have to follow His directions.

We have to be completely devoted to our relationship with God being our life's priority. Not our top priority, our only priority. Because when our relationship with God is right the other important areas of our lives will automatically fall into place. We'll be the type of spouse, parent, son/daughter, church member, employee, or friend that God wants us to be. How intense is your study and prayer life? Our relationship with God is based off communication just like any other relationship. Us reading and studying His word is Him talking to us and prayer is us talking to Him. Do you pray everyday but only study His word once or twice a week? How would you feel in a relationship if you did all the listening but only spoke to the other person once or twice a week? If you wouldn't he happy with that then why would our God and Father be happy with that? We feed ourselves physical food multiple times a day to nourish a body that will deteriorate no matter what. Do we feed ourselves spiritually to nourish the body that will live forever? We spend hours throughout the week on our hobbies or entertainment but can we spend those hours growing in God's word? How much spiritual growth do you get that's not related to going to church during the week? When you're at work or school do the people you come in contact with on a consistent basis know you're a servant and follower of Christ? Are you living your life so that you can go to heaven or just so you don't go to hell? The end result may be the same but the motives that drive our actions are different. God loves us and He has told us how to show our love back to Him by faithful loving obedience. As long as we're consistent with that we'll be able to handle Him saying no to our prayers because we'll know He still knows what's best for us. And if God says something is best for us, we can always trust that He's right.

Printed in the United States
By Bookmasters